FOOD and DRINK

A Pictorial Archive from Nineteenth-Century Sources

Selected by
JIM HARTER

SECOND REVISED EDITION

Dover Publications, Inc.
New York

CONTENTS

Published in Canada by General Publishing Company, Ltd., 30 Lesmill Road, Don Mills, Toronto, Ontario.

Published in the United Kingdom by Constable and Company, Ltd., 10 Orange Street, London WC2H 7EG.

Food and Drink: A Pictorial Archive from Nineteenth-Century Sources is a new work, first published by Dover Publications, Inc., in 1979. Second revised edition published 1980.

DOVER *Pictorial Archive* SERIES

International Standard Book Number: 0-486-23816-4
Library of Congress Catalog Card Number: 79-50498

Manufactured in the United States of America
Dover Publications, Inc.
180 Varick Street
New York, N.Y. 10014

PUBLISHER'S NOTE

Wood engravings, with their crisp black-and-white lines, were popularized by Thomas Bewick at the end of the eighteenth century and quickly became the favored medium of mass reproduction of artwork in the nineteenth. While there were only about 20 wood engravers in the United States in 1838, by 1870 their number had swelled to about 400. Most of them earned their living by engraving illustrations for the great periodicals of the era, *Harper's Weekly* and *Leslie's Illustrated* foremost among them. With great skill the artists rendered sketches and photographs into precise illustrations. The medium admitted a wide variety of styles from simple, bold line drawings to those so carefully worked that the effect of gradation of tone was achieved, sometimes with an impressionistic feeling.

By the mid-1880s the means had become available for reproducing photographs as halftone illustrations, but they were both crude and expensive. It was not until the 1890s that the art of wood engraving began to be superseded by the new process. Ironically, now that the technique of the wood engraving has been largely lost, the popularity of these illustrations is reviving. Artists find the material widely adaptable to projects such as collage. Graphic designers are rediscovering how well the engravings complement typography.

Using his keen eye, artist Jim Harter has culled this selection from issues of *Harper's, Leslie's, The* [London] *Graphic, The London Illustrated News* and other periodicals and books. He has chosen the material to reflect both the diversity of the subject and the variety of styles of wood engraving. Exercising his prerogative as an artist, Mr. Harter has also included a few illustrations that predate the nineteenth century, as well as some that were done in media other than the wood engraving. The entire selection has been made to be of maximum use to artists and designers by including as many aspects of food and eating as possible. Raw meats, fish, fowl, game, fruits and vegetables are depicted, as are kitchen and dining utensils, kitchen scenes, scenes of eating merely as a means of survival, warm family dinners and grand banquets in which food, although costly and magnificently prepared, serves merely as a ceremonial framework.

MENU

Menu

MENU

MENU

MENU

MENU

MENU

Carte du Jour

MENU

Menu

CAFÉ

MENU

MENU

M

MENU

CAFÉ

CAFÉ

CARTE du JOUR

Meisenbach.

Meisenbach.

A la cart

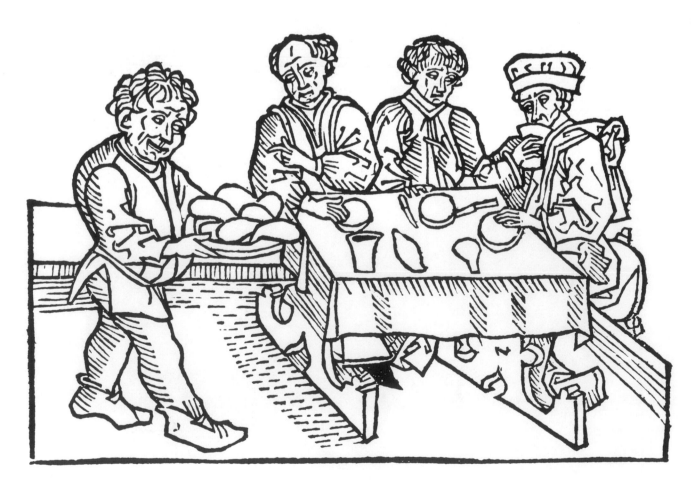

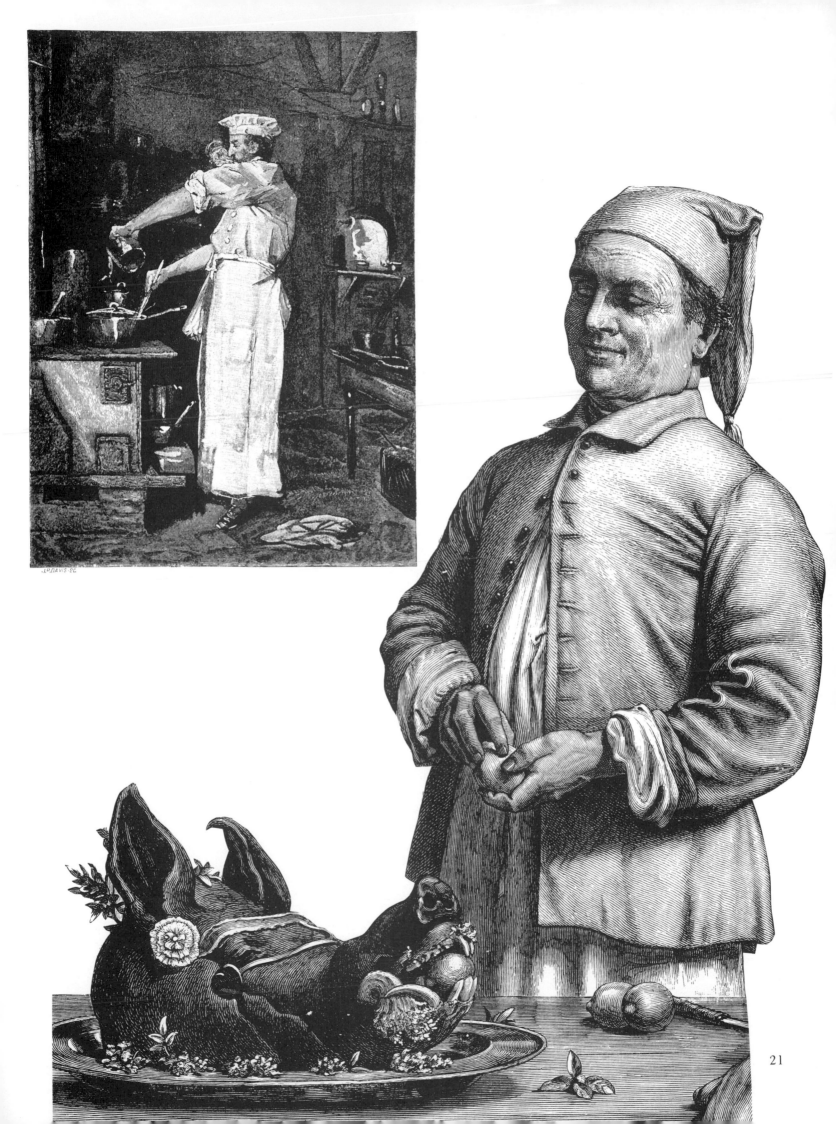

Dessiné par J. M. Moreau le Jeune.

Gravé par Helman

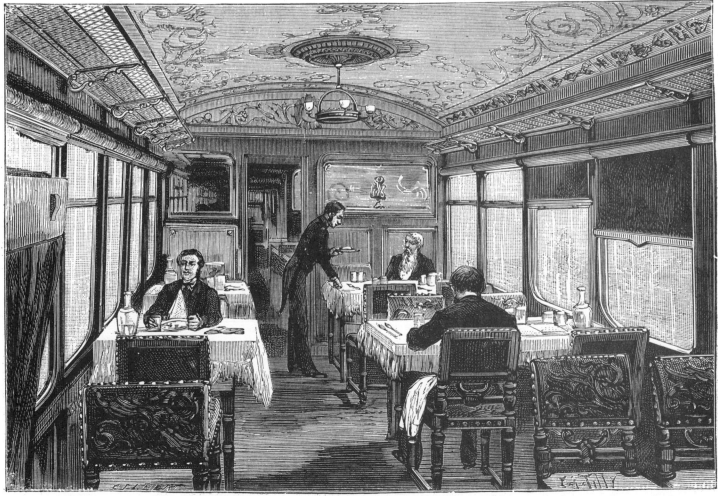

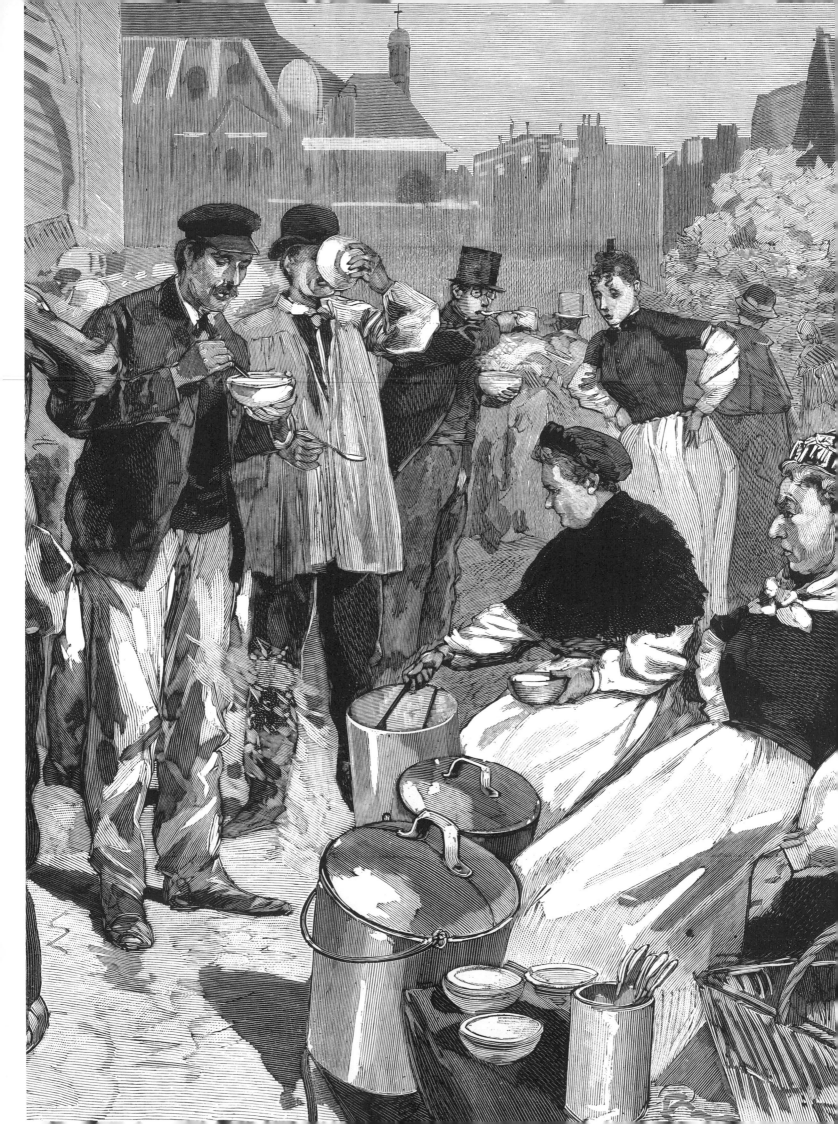

DELIKATESSEN

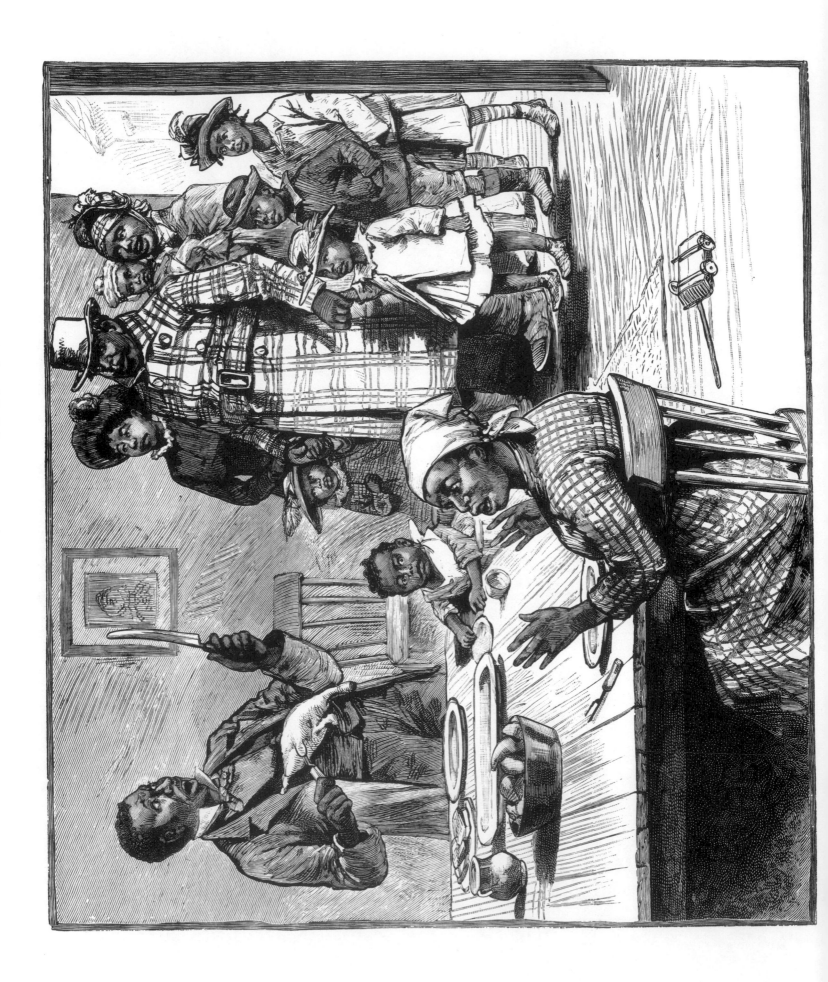

6895 75c

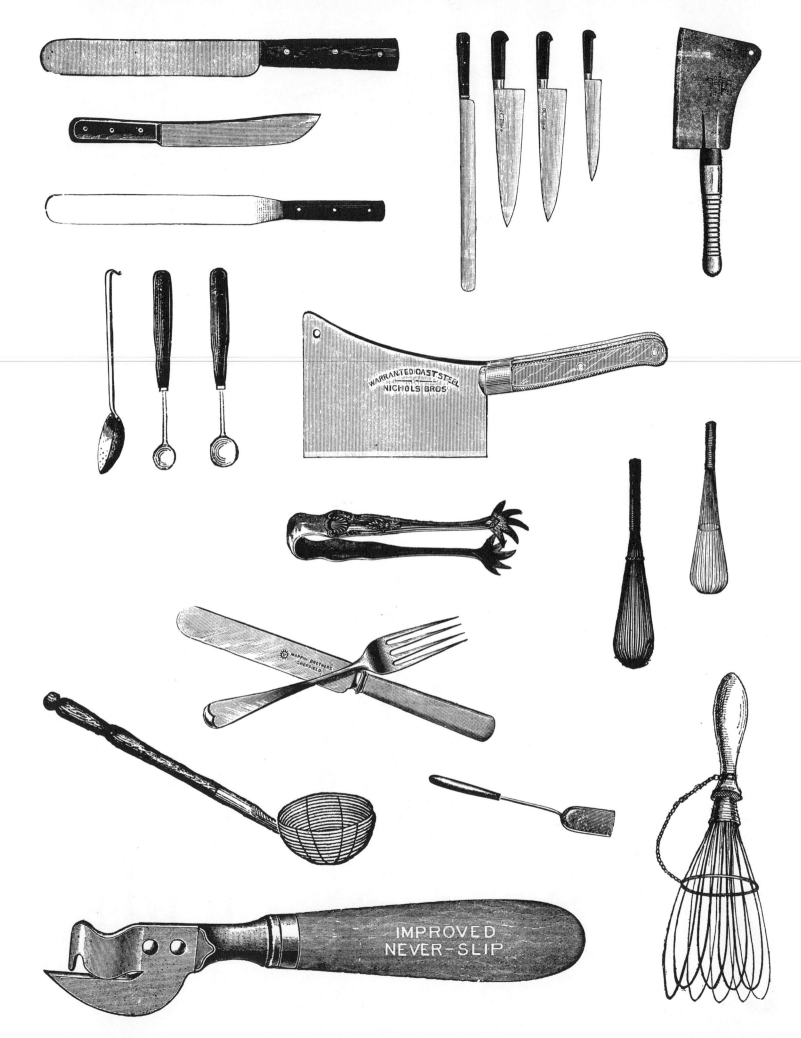

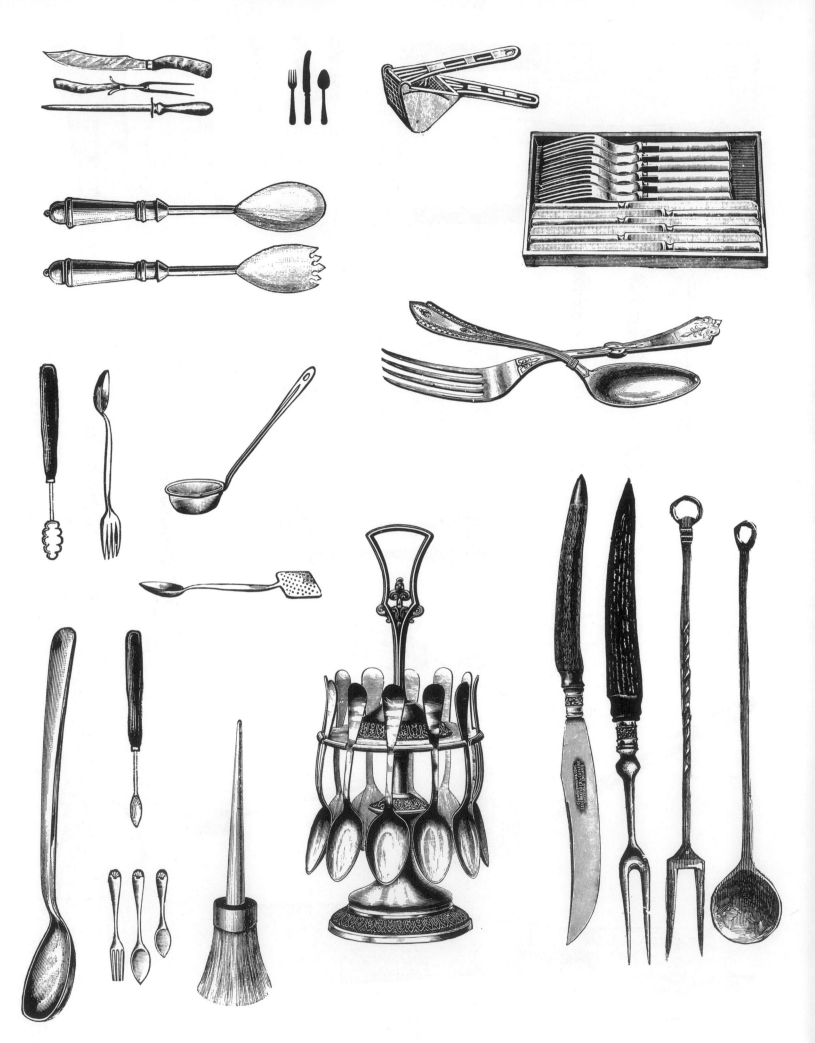

OUR
BEST

CORNED BEEF

CORNED BEEF

CORNED
BEEF

COMPRESSED
COOKED

CORNED BEEF

POTTED
CHICKEN

POTTED
HAM

POTTED
TONGUE

POTTED
HAM

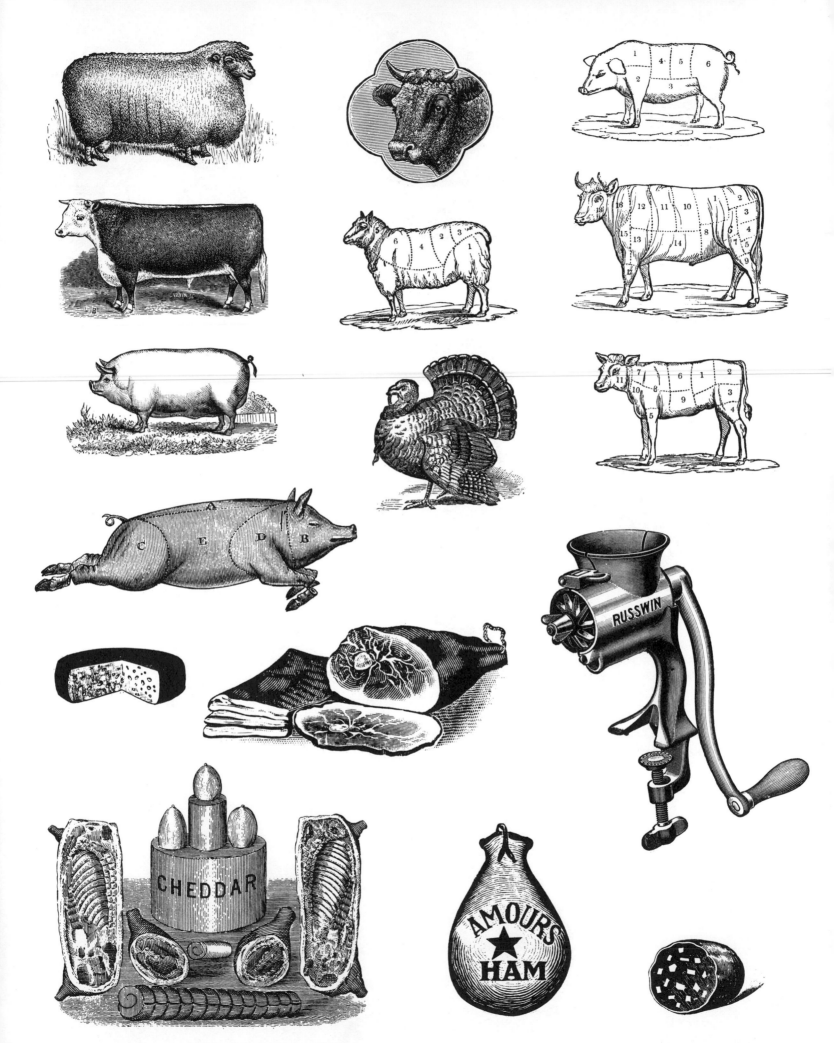

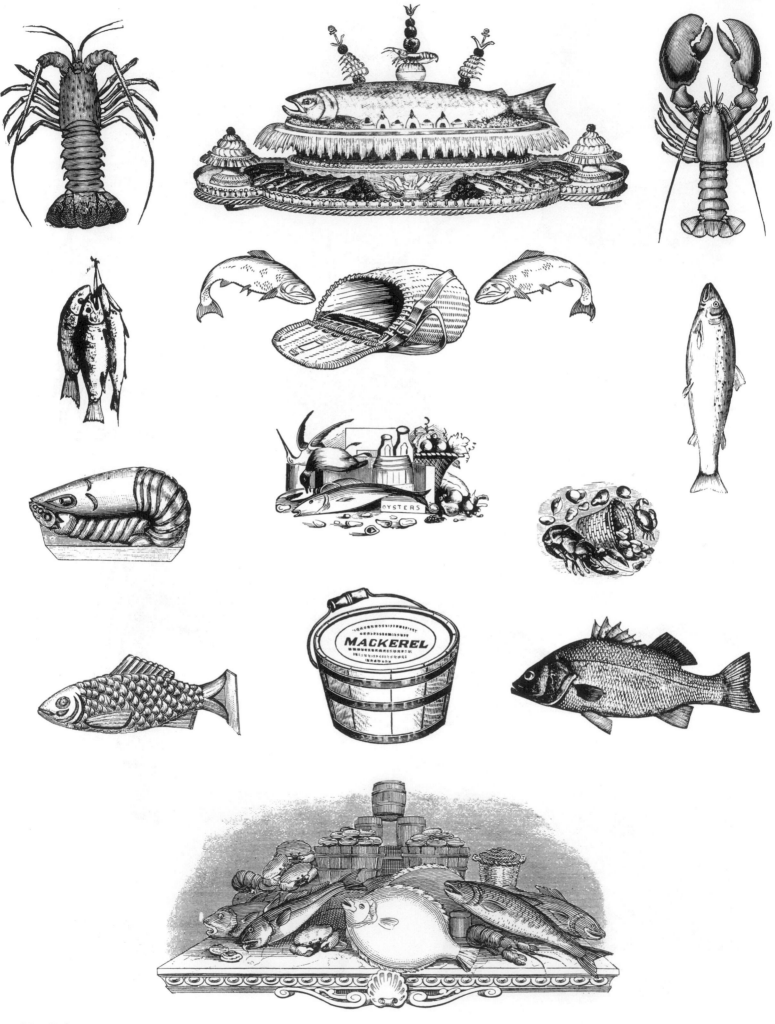

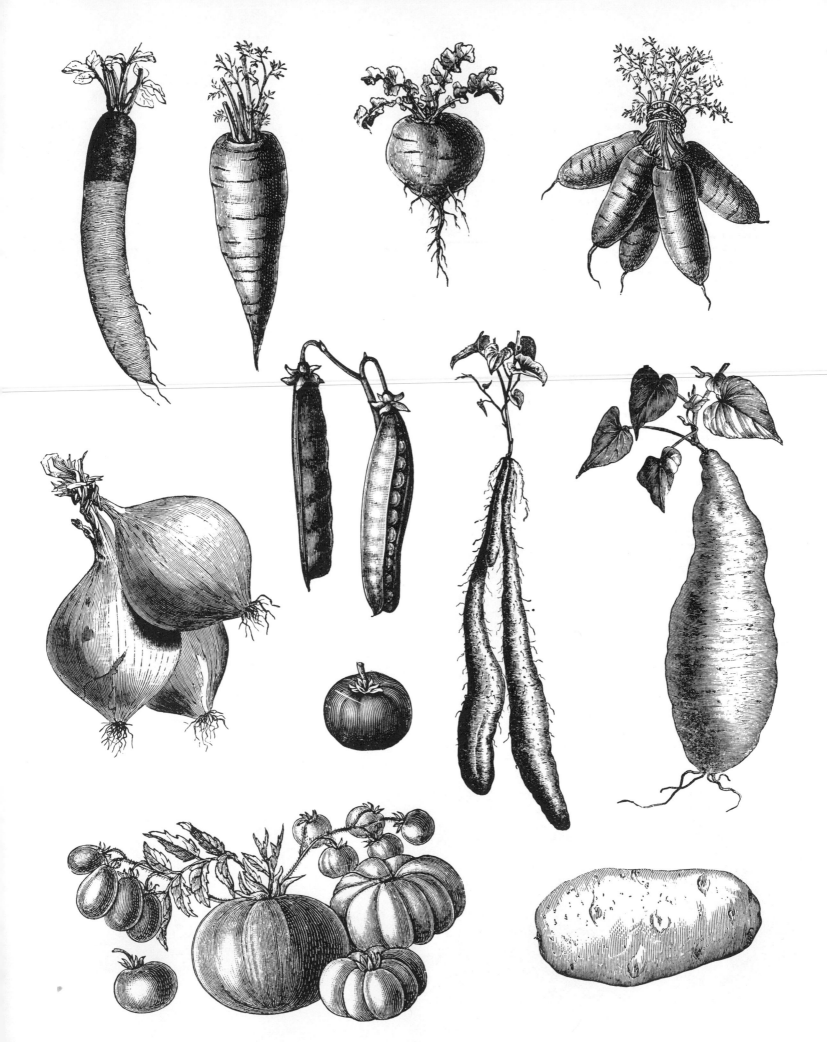

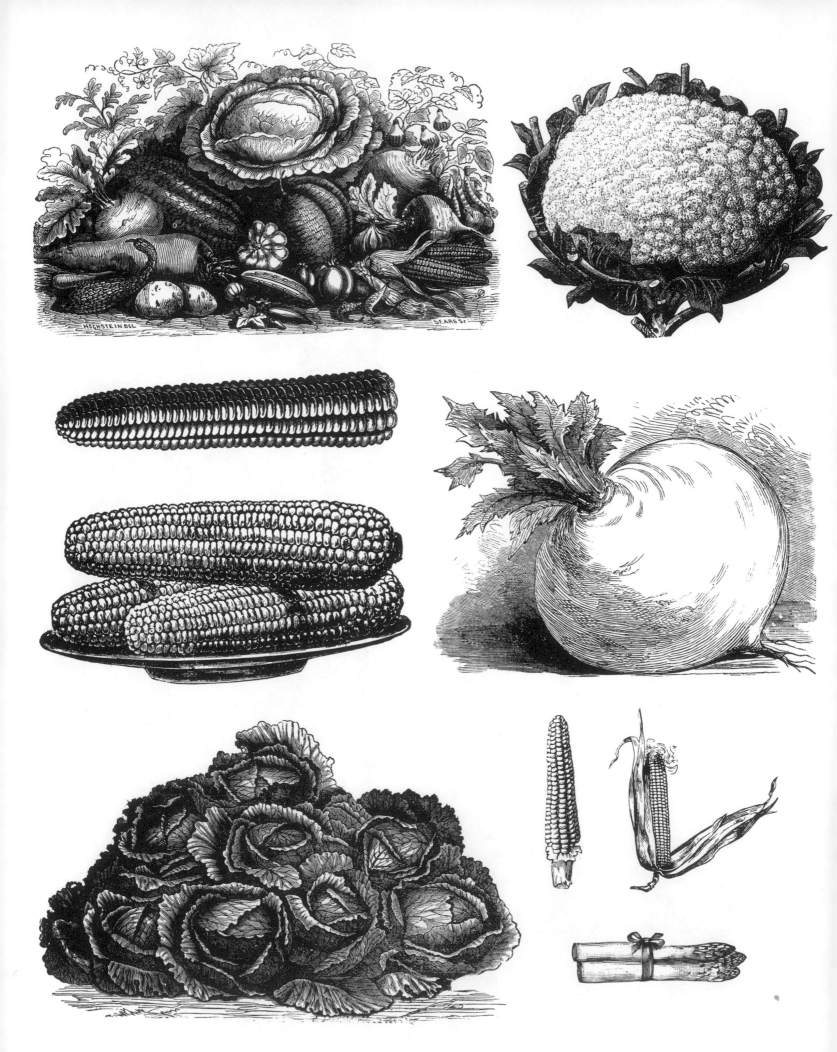

90 *Fruit*

ROOT BEER

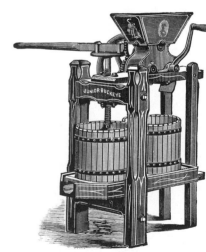

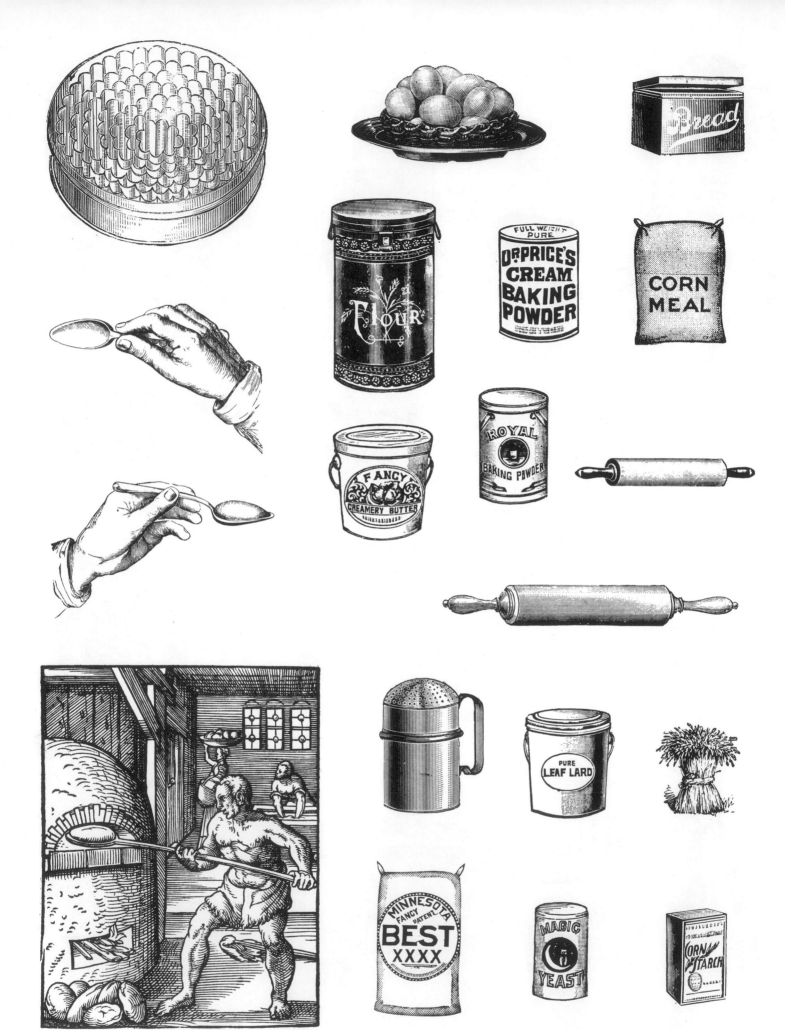

TEAS
GENUINE
AS
IMPORTED

FRESH
TEAS

TEA'S READY.

DELICIOUS!

MAZAWATTEE
A HIGH CLASS TEA
FROM THE SWEET SCENTED ISLAND
CEYLON
THE MOST LUSCIOUS TEA IN THE WORLD

SIR M A SHEE PR.A PINXT

VERNON SCULP

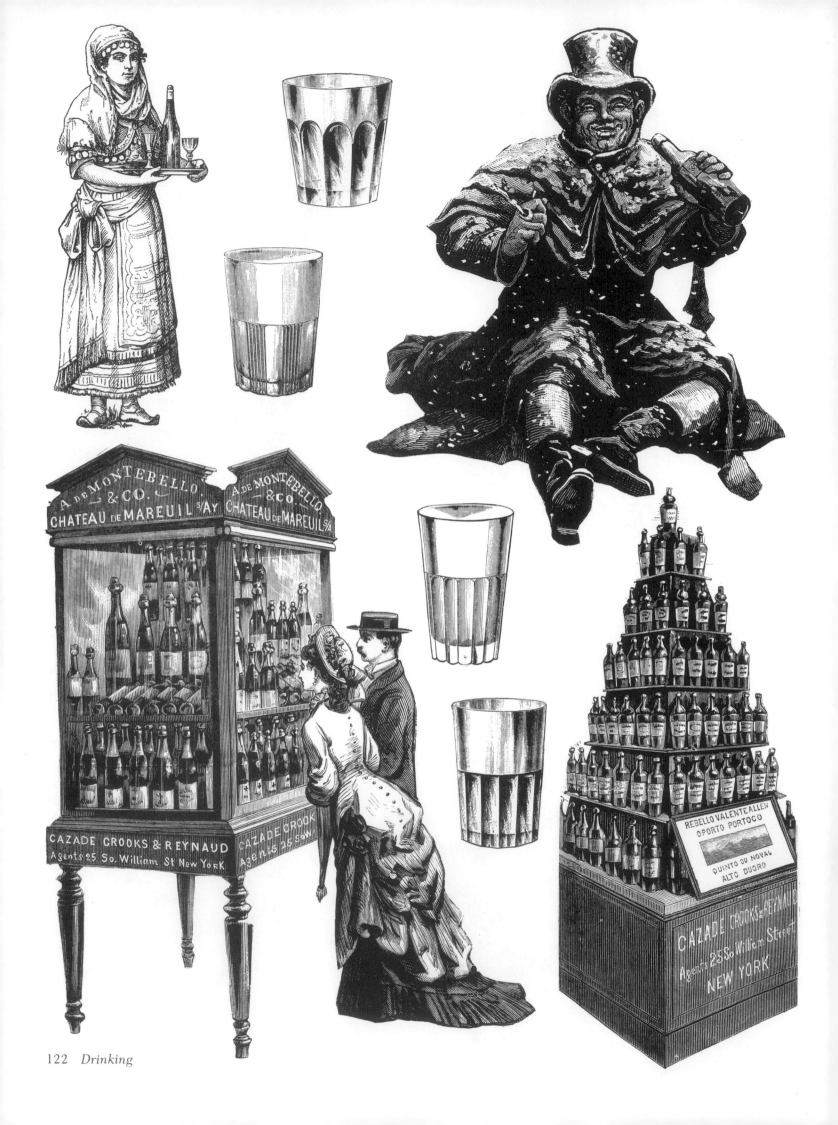

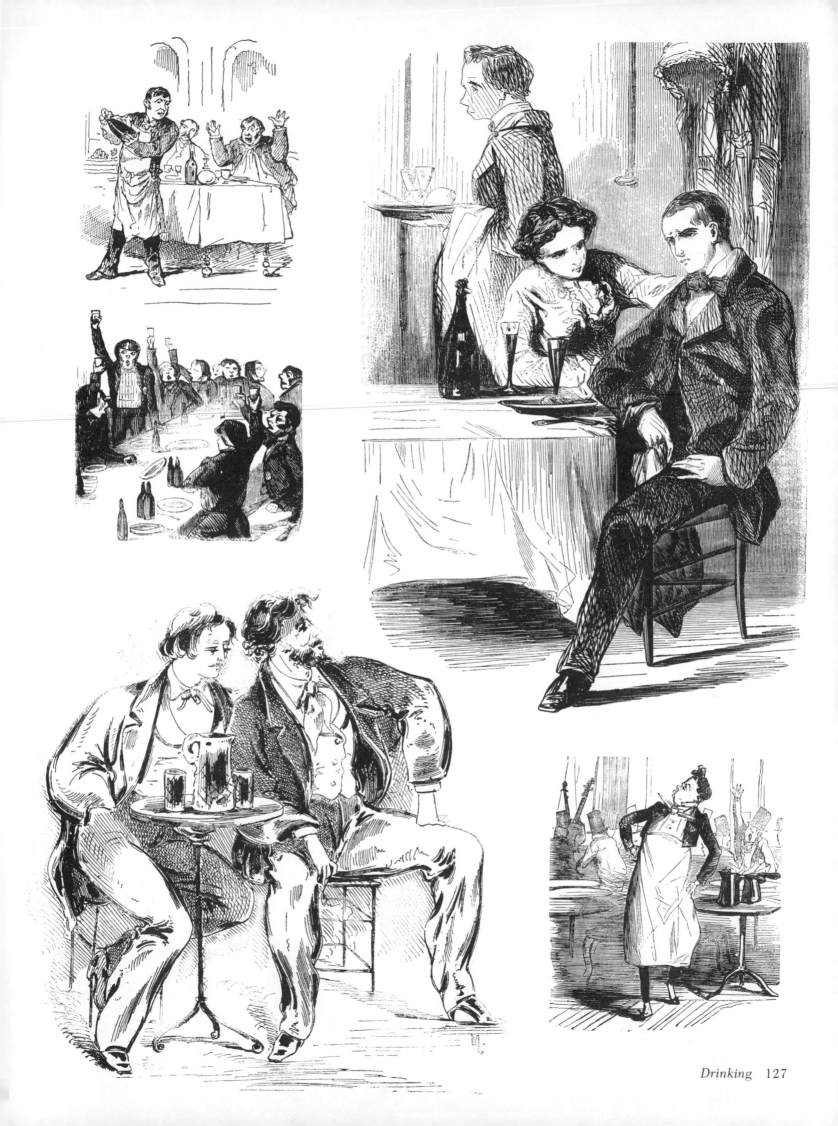

"YOU'LL NEVER MISS THE WATER"

LAGER

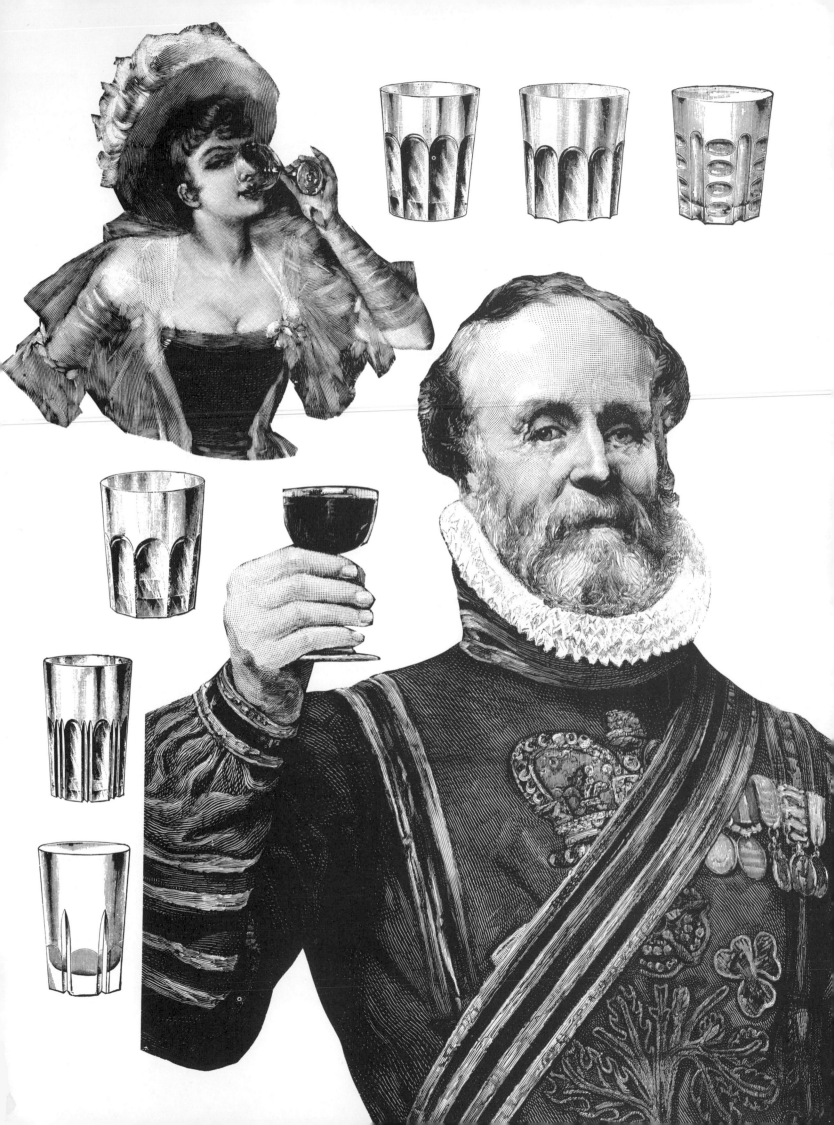